The Deep Green Planet

THE CONIFEROUS FOREST

The Deep Green Planet

THE CONIFEROUS FOREST

RENATO MASSA AND MONICA CARABELLA

ENGLISH TRANSLATION BY TRANSPERFECT TRANSLATIONS, INC.

RSVP

RAINTREE STECK-VAUGHN
PUBLISHERS
The Steck-Vaughn Company

Austin, Texas

Published by Raintree Steck-Vaughn Publishers, an imprint of Steck-Vaughn Company

Editors
Caterina Longanesi, Linda Zierdt-Warshaw

Design and layout
Jaca Book Graphics Department

Library of Congress Cataloging-in-Publication Data

Massa, Renato.
    [Foresta dei giganti. English]
    The coniferous forest / Renato Massa and Monica Carabella.
       p.   cm. — (The Deep green planet)
    Summary: Discusses the different types of coniferous forests found all over the world and the animals living there.
    Includes bibliographical references (p.57) and index.
    ISBN 0-8172-4313-5
    1. Forest ecology — Juvenile literature.   2. Conifers — Ecology — Juvenile literature.
3. Forest animals — Juvenile literature.   4. Forest plants — Juvenile literature.   [1. Forest ecology.   2. Ecology.   3. Conifers.   4. Forest animals.   5. Forest plants.]   I. Carabella, Monica.   II. Series.
QH541.5.F6M3813   1997
574.5'2642 — dc20   96–38414
                                            CIP   AC

Printed and bound in the United States
1 2 3 4 5 6 7 8 9 0 WO 99 98 97

CONTENTS

INTRODUCTION

Ancient Norse tales lead us into dark forests of pyramid-shaped trees. When the snow and the frost do not cover everything like a magic dust, large and colorful mushrooms grow in "fairy rings" within clearings. Scented carpets of flowers attract swarms of insects. Even in the depths of winter, the seemingly constant silence can be shattered by the high, scratchy voice of a nutcracker or a flock of chattering birds. With the sorrowful call of the bullfinch and the rhythmic song of the titmouse, the forest is changed from a dark and enchanted place into a home for friendly sprites.

The northern forests are vast and uniform. Over a broad area of Europe, Asia, and North America, they have a similar appearance, with a few species of majestic trees of almost equal height and a limited number of widely dispersed animals. Coniferous forests are the opposite of tropical forests. The northern forests are as cold and dry as the tropical forests are warm and wet. Over vast areas, the northern forests show little variety, while the tropical forests are quite diverse. A single species of goshawk dominates, as does a single Eurasian eagle owl, a single hawk owl, a single species of elk, or wolverine. Other animals, such as the nutcracker and the lynx, show small variations full of colorful accents. If the tropical forest is the kingdom of fantasy and freedom, the world of the conifers is dominated by harsh necessity. Everything is planned and organized down to the smallest detail to allow the continuation of the few forms of life that seem to have survived in an almost exhaustive fashion.

But wherever something special occurs, as in the North American fog belt, unexpected possibilities open up and produce extraordinary events. The giant conifers, designed by biological evolution to survive stubbornly dry conditions, have the ability to absorb large amounts of water from fog and mist. Thus, they continue growing to a huge size, collecting water ever more efficiently to produce an extraordinary natural occurrence: a forest of giants. It is an occurrence unique in the world that recalls the ancient Norse legends in a modern and real form.

RENATO MASSA

CHARACTERISTICS OF CONIFERS

MALE CONES

FEMALE CONES

Female Pinecones and Male Pinecones

The term **conifer** identifies **gymnosperms** that have the female flower cluster in the form of a cone. This part of the plant is usually called a pinecone. A pinecone, or **strobilus** as botanists call it, has a woody texture and takes several months to mature. It is made up of **scales**, under which are two well-protected seeds. Only a few conifers, such as the **juniper** and the European **yew**, produce single seeds that are not in cones. Instead, they are enclosed in a fleshy covering called a **pseudodrupe**. A pseudodrupe is a **false fruit** that is similar to a berry.

In gymnosperms, the strobili, or seed-bearing structures, are the female pinecones. Male pinecones are much smaller and grow on the tips of the branches, alone or in groups. They are short-lived, lasting only long enough to spread large amounts of **pollen**. The pollen, with the help of the wind and special structures that act as parachutes, fertilizes the female cones of other trees.

Most conifers bear both male and female flowers on the same tree. These plants are therefore **monoecious** or **hermaphroditic**. In some cases, such as the European yew, individual trees are of separate sexes, or **dioecious**. In either case, the male flowers and the female flowers mature at different times to prevent **self-fertilization**, which could be harmful to the survival of the species.

Needle-Shaped Leaves

Conifers include such different trees as the silver fir, also known as the Christmas tree,

the broad, umbrella-shaped cluster pines, the slender cypresses, the huge **sequoias**, and the twisted shrublike junipers. The range of variation within this **order** is very large. The evolutionary success of these **evergreen** trees is shown by the large **coniferous forests** that thrive all over the world. Most of these forests exist in the cold and **temperate zones**. But a few forests thrive, to a lesser extent, in tropical and subtropical climates.

The most obvious trait of the conifers is their needle-shaped or scaly leaves. These leaves are very well adapted to survive harsh climates that have extreme variations in temperature and long dry periods. They can survive these conditions because of the small surfaces of the needles and a thick, waxy coating that acts as insulation.

Almost all conifers are evergreen plants. They can carry out **photosynthesis** and draw water from the ground all year, even when

1. On the left, a branch of a pine tree with male pinecones, which contain the pollen. On the right, a branch with female cones in different stages of maturity. The pollen grains are carried by the wind to the female gametophyte, which is enclosed in the ovule. The sperm produced by the germinating pollen grains are transported into the ovule by the pollen tube. After fertilization, the ovule changes into a seed that contains the embryo of the new plant, a cover, and various nutritional substances.

2

4

2. Male flowers and
(3.) spruce sapling,
Picea pungens.
4. Male flowers and
(5.) pinecone of *Pinus
nigra*. In the spring,
the pollen of conifers
is carried by the wind,
usually in large
quantities. It is spread
in dense clouds over
several days so that
the pollen is likely to
encounter a female
flower.

3   5

the temperature is very low. Their trunks act as storage tanks for large amounts of water, **mineral salts**, and **carbohydrates**, such as sugars. All these substances are useful in various ways for helping the trees survive their harsh surroundings.

Another advantage of conifers is the fact that they do not have to replace their leaves as often as **broadleaf trees**. In fact, only 15 percent of the conifer's leaves are replaced each year. This contrasts sharply with **deciduous broadleaf trees**, which replace all their leaves year after year. In addition, the compact shape of conifer leaves allows these trees to use the **nutrients** in their leaves more

1. The supercontinent Pangea began to break up in the Jurassic period, 140 to 210 million years ago. At that time, the climate was still warm. The Earth was covered by conifers, such as spruces, firs, monkey puzzle trees, and sequoias, and by other primitive plants. **2.** The dinosaurs were still abundant, although there had been a first wave of extinctions as early as in the late Triassic period. New groups of mammals and lizards were beginning to appear. At the end of the Jurassic period, the earliest birds with a long vertebral column, teeth, and claws on their wings, such as the famous *Archaeopteryx* that is shown in flight in the drawing, began to appear.

efficiently than do broadleaf trees. The small size provides a shorter path for liquids that have to be transported. This guarantees them greater efficiency.

Trees Shaped Like Pyramids

The shape of conifers is also an **adaptation** that guarantees the most exposure to sunlight. The pyramid shape of most conifers allows the trees to absorb the sun's rays, even when they strike at low angles or pass through clouds. The shapes of many conifers, such as those of the genera *Tsuga* and *Abies*, which live in exceptionally cloudy areas, also make it possible for the trees to rapidly shed snow that builds up on their branches, whose downward slant forms a sort of chute. The rapid shedding of the snowy blanket allows the tree to resume photosynthesis almost immediately. It also keeps the branches from breaking under the excess weight of accumulated snow.

Finally, the conifers, which not only survive but thrive in poor soils and harsh climates, have an additional weapon to defend themselves against animal and plant **parasites**. They contain protective substances, such as the **terpenes** and **tannins** that make up their well-known **resins**, that discourage many insects, **fungi**, and other undesirable intruders from boring into their tissues.

MONTEREY CYPRESS
Cupressus macrocarpa
(Cupressaceae)

NORTH
AMERICA

REDWOOD
Sequoia sempervirens
(Taxodiaceae)

BALD CYPRESS
Taxodium distichum
(Taxodiaceae)

SOUTH
AMERICA

TAIGA

MOUNTAIN FOREST

COLD, TEMPERATE
RAIN FOREST

MEDITERRANEAN
VEGETATION

WARM, TEMPERATE
RAIN FOREST

MONKEY PUZZLE
Araucaria araucana
(Araucariaceae)

Worldwide distribution of conifers. Examples of all the families are shown except the Taxaceae. Compared to the angiosperms, there are not many families. The family that includes the most species is the Pinaceae.

NORWAY SPRUCE
Picea abies
(Pinaceae)

EUROPEAN LARCH
Larix decidua
(Pinaceae)

EUROPE

ASIA

AFRICA

JAPANESE CEDAR
Cryptomeria japonica
(Taxodiaceae)

AUSTRALIA

UMBRELLA PINE
Pinus pinea
(Pinaceae)

PODOCARP
Podocarpus
(Podocarpaceae)

CEDAR OF
LEBANON
Cedrus libani
(Pinaceae)

THE LARGE NORTHERN FORESTS

The Earth's large forests of conifers extend mostly over the Northern Hemisphere, across North America, Europe, and Asia. They cover approximately 15 percent of Earth's land surface. In most regions covered by these forests, which are called by their Siberian name **taiga**, summers are short, and winters are long and harsh.

What **ecologists** define as the "biome of Northern Hemisphere coniferous forests" is a broad band between 45 and 75 degrees north **latitude**. Here, the characteristics of the climate have forced plants to make special adaptations to most efficiently use the brief periods of mild temperatures and survive the long, bitterly cold winters.

The upper latitudes' limit of the coniferous forest consists of open **tundra**. The tundra has no trees. So the taiga is exposed to frequent invasions from masses of cold arctic air. These air masses travel swiftly because there are no mountain chains to block their path and because the **topographical slope** of Earth descends toward the pole.

2

1. The map shows the extent of glaciation in North America. The numbers indicate how long ago in thousands of years the glaciations took place. The most recent major glaciation, called the Wisconsin glacial stage, occurred 17,000 to 19,000 years ago. *P* indicates glaciations prior to the Wisconsin.
2. Face of the Columbia glacier, in Alaska
3. Coniferous forests on the high plains cut by the Grand Canyon, in Arizona. Their adaptation to dry conditions allows conifers to live in the north, where the water is trapped as ice for many months of the year, and in dry zones on the boundary between the temperate and subtropical zones.

3

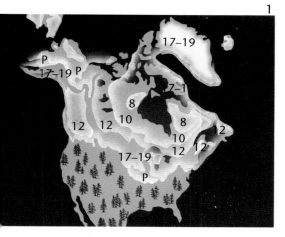

An additional factor that limits the area occupied by the coniferous forests is the condition of the soil. The permanently frozen permafrost layer makes it difficult for roots to penetrate far into the ground. So trees of the coniferous forest often have shallow roots that spread out widely to take maximum advantage of the moisture in the upper levels of the ground, which only thaw occasionally.

Within the general characteristics of the belt of coniferous forests, the climate conditions in different regions vary within certain limits. Notable differences can be seen in types of forest vegetation going from south to north and from lower to higher altitudes at the same latitude. While the various forests are adapted to the dry conditions, their characteristic species change.

In North America, Europe, and western Siberia, the Norway spruce (*Picea*), the silver

4. A pine tree at the bottom of the Grand Canyon. Conifers spread easily over the mountain slopes, because the dispersal of their seeds is aided by birds, such as the nutcracker, which stores pinecones in hiding places. The bird carries the cones over long distances and hides them in many different locations.

5. A *Pinus longaeva* in the snow-covered winter landscape of Bryce Canyon, in Utah.

fir (*Abies*), and various types of pine trees (*Pinus*) flourish. In Central and eastern Siberia, the most common is the **larch** (*Larix*), a conifer that differs from all others because it loses its needles in the winter. In North America and east Asia, there are various species of the genera *Tsuga* and *Pseudotsuga*. Some broadleaf trees that grow mixed in with these large coniferous forests are the **ash, aspen,** birch, and dwarf willow. All these trees grow rapidly in open spaces near water or in areas where recent forest fires have occurred.

Poor Soils

Over the past million years, the greater part of the area that is now occupied by the northern coniferous forests has been subjected to much glacial activity. The glaciers have left behind many depressions with poor **drainage** as evidence of their presence. That is why the large Nordic forests often have

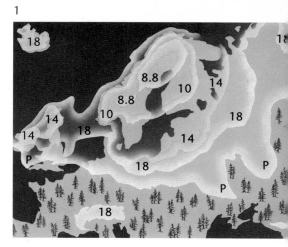

1. The maximum extent of the glaciers in Europe during the most recent glacial stage, called the Würm glacial stage, occurred 18,000 years ago. Before that, the glaciers had reached even farther south (P).
2. View of Lake Teletskoye in the Siberian taiga, in Russia. The taiga, the realm of the conifers, is one of the largest natural environments on the planet. It still covers millions of square kilometers.
3. Alpine lake **4.** Steep cliffs alongside a stream in the forest of Derborance, in Switzerland

thousands of small lakes and swampy areas.

In these areas, the **underbrush** is not very dense. Besides having to overcome the problems created by the permafrost soil, the lower vegetation layers must compete with taller plants for light and make do with soil that is very poor in nutrients. The soil in these forests is subject to **podzolization**. Podzolization is a geological process typical of **subarctic** climates. **Podzol** soils are not very fertile because of a continuous loss of

magnesium, potassium, and phosphorus. These **alkaline** substances are mostly taken from the lower layers of the soil. This results in the acidification of the soil, limiting the variety of the plants that can grow in the underbrush. Finally, the needles that do fall to the ground contain almost no water or nutritional elements, because conifers recover everything useful from their needles before shedding them. In a way, conifers are programmed to take back most of the useful

5. The silver fir (*Abies alba*) grows in the forests of north-central Europe, often alongside the beech.

6. Branches and cones of *Pinus wallichiana*, an Asiatic species that grows from Afghanistan to Nepal

7. Branches and mature cones of the weeping spruce (*Picea breweriana*), a species of red spruce that grows in the western forests of North America, from Oregon to California

8. A North American conifer (*Pseudotsuga menziesii*) is one of the tallest trees in the

basic minerals and the presence of **moraine** deposits and large irregular rocks. Because of the low temperatures, **organic** material that falls to the ground decomposes slowly. This keeps nutrients, such as nitrogen and **phosphorus**, from being recycled.

Soils in coniferous forests have another problem, too. Conifers **acidify** the soil on which they live because they take in and retain several basic elements, such as **calcium,**

substances from their needles in preparation for shutting down the needles' life cycle. As a result, the underbrush of coniferous forests is characterized by a relatively small number of species. These species are very well adapted to the soil conditions and very abundant. They include **whortleberries**, junipers, wild roses, and dwarf willows, along with numerous **mosses**, lichens, and ferns.

world. It can grow to a height of more than 122 meters (400 feet).

9. Norway spruce (*Picea abies*), a common European species frequently used as a Christmas tree

10. Austrian pine (*Pinus nigra*), a Eurasian and North African species that also grows in very dense groups, although it can still receive a large amount of light from above

11. The arolla or Swiss pine (*Pinus cembra*), a species adapted to the cold moraine forest of Aletsch, Switzerland

12. The European larch (*Larix decidua*) is among the few species of conifers that lose their leaves in the winter.

13. The European larch in the summer

CONIFERS IN WARM CLIMATES

The northern forest holds the largest group of conifers on the planet. However, it is not the only group of conifers that exists. Rock pines and cypresses provide shade along the Mediterranean coast, and junipers decorate Mediterranean beaches. Yews, cedars, monkey puzzle trees, and evergreens spread their branches in many of the large city parks of central Europe.

The unusual bald cypress (*Taxodium*) grows with its roots submerged in shallow water along the banks of rivers and lakes in Europe, and in some coastal areas of the southern United States and Mexico. The bald cypress is characteristic of the landscape of marshy areas that have many small, isolated islands, called **everglades**. The bald cypress also has one feature that is unique in its class and gives it an unusual appearance. It has developed special submerged roots that function as respiratory organs. The roots, called **pneumatophores**, look like little steeples sticking up out of the water in the marshes around the trees. The pneumatophores are cylindrical organs that stand several centimeters above the surface of the water. They are comparable to the respiratory organs of the **mangrove** tree, another plant that grows in swampy environments.

The roots of the bald cypress form extensive tangled masses, **buttresses** partly buried in the ground. They stick out and look like stumps. Unmoving, massive, and mysterious in the mists of the everglades, the bald cypresses, or swamp cypresses, grow to heights of 40 to 50 meters (130 to 150 feet). The trunks have diameters of 4 to 5 meters (13 to 16 feet) and are frequently blanketed in mosses, ferns, vines, and **epiphytes**. In many city parks of Europe, the bald cypress is sometimes seen growing on the shores of ponds where, when fully grown, their respiratory organs stick out of the water, creating quite an unusual sight.

The *Podocarpus* evergreens are conifers that are no less remarkable than the bald cypress. There are more than a hundred species of these trees. They grow throughout the mountainous regions in the Southern Hemisphere of Asia, Africa, and South America and in the tropics and **subtropics**. These evergreens, which grow either as shrubs or trees, are characterized by special

1. Close-up of the scale leaves of the Japanese cedar (*Cryptomeria japonica*). The tree is a large member of the Taxodiaceae family, originally from Japan and southeast China, where it grows in vast forests.
2. The same family includes the swamp cypress (*Taxodium distichum*), a conifer common in the Florida Everglades.
3. Branches of typical flat needles of the European yew (*Taxus baccata*, family Taxaceae). The fruits of the yew are beautiful red "berries," although they are actually strobili, or pinecones.
4. Branches, trunk, cone, foliage, and leaves of *Araucaria bidwillii*, a native of Australia. The *Auraucaria*, which include the monkey puzzles, are ancient conifers. They are considered to be among the "living fossils" of the plant kingdom. In the Jurassic period, 140 to 210 million years ago, they covered vast areas of North America. Today, they survive in nature only in the Southern Hemisphere.

4

seeds. Instead of developing in cones, as in pines and firs, the seeds are enclosed in an edible, fleshy shell that is shaped like a cup. The seed covering is similar to the **aril** of the European yew.

The **outgrowths** of the seeds of *Podocarpus* evergreens are formed by a swelling of the **petiole** and the modified, scaly leaves typical of conifers. They do not originate from the **ovary**, as do the **true fruits** of the **angiosperms**. Some species of *Podocarpus* evergreens are grown to make jams and jellies from the pulp of these false fruits.

Also widespread, especially in mountainous areas of the warm and temperate climates of the Mediterranean basin, is another type of conifer: the cedar. The cedars are popular in gardens all over Europe, where they were imported for the first time in the sixteenth century. In ancient times, these majestic trees with their spectacular canopies and massive trunks were cut for lumber. The lumber was used to construct buildings, to decorate temples and palaces, and to carve statues for the homes of the wealthy.

The four known species of true cedars live in northern Africa, on the island of Cyprus, in the Middle East, and in the Himalayas. The cedar forests around the Mediterranean grow on the slopes of dry and otherwise barren hills, and have little underbrush. The Himalayan cedars thrive in climates that vary greatly over a vast area.

Cedars live for many years but take a long time to reach an age where they can reproduce. A cedar tree does not produce seeds before it is 40 or 50 years old. The wide but discontinuous distribution of these conifers reflects their ancient abundance and the continuous shrinkage of their territory. Their shrinking territory is due to changing climate conditions and competition with the more successful angiosperms, which are more highly evolved and adaptable.

1. Branch with **(a.)** leaves, **(b.)** flowers, and **(c.)** seeds of the podocarp *(Podocarpus neriifolius)*, a conifer of the Himalayan region. Other species of podocarps are found in tropical areas of Asia, Africa, and South America.

2. Fruit-bearing branches of the savin or red juniper *(Juniperus sabina)*, a Mediterranean species that grows either as a tree or a shrub to a height of 8 to 9 meters (25 to 30 feet). In general, the junipers are small, but some tropical species are giants.

3., and 5. Moroccan cedar *(Cedrus atlantica)*, a beautiful species that grows up to 45 meters (150 feet) tall. It grows in magnificent forests on the slopes of the Atlas Mountains (shown in the insert),

although these forests are rapidly being destroyed. A similar species, the Cedar of Lebanon, was used to build the famous Temple of Jerusalem, but only a few examples of the tree survive on some mountain slopes in Lebanon.

4. Stone pine or umbrella pine *(Pinus pinea)*, a characteristic Mediterranean species with abundant, umbrella-shaped foliage that truly beautifies the coast of central Italy.

THE GIANTS OF THE FOREST

1

Sequoia fossils

Metasequoia fossils

The Trees of the Fog Belt
Along the Pacific coast of North America is an area known locally as the "fog belt." The climate and environmental conditions of the area have led to the formation of a coniferous forest having unique characteristics. Here, from central California to Alaska, there is very little precipitation. However, a thick and persistent fog more than makes up for the lack of rainfall. It has been calculated that the fog in this region can provide water in quantities that are two or three times greater than the local annual precipitation, assuming that the trees can intercept this moisture. It is this need to take advantage of the fog that explains the tendency toward the gigantic size shown by the conifers of this region. In fact, in addition to capturing moisture from the persistent fogs, the large plants also intercept the fleeting coastal fog as it drifts inland. The droplets of water in the fog condense on the tops of these trees. Then condensation falls as a fine drizzle from the **canopy**.

The forests of the fog belt are **temperate rain forests**. In southern California, the immense sequoias dominate. These truly special trees are classified in the family of the Taxodiaceae, which is one of ancient origin.

The existence of conifers at such low latitudes is a unique phenomenon. It probably reflects the strange geo-climatic conditions of this region. For a long time, the slopes of the coastal mountain chains and the Cascades have captured and stopped the flow of moisture-laden clouds coming from the Pacific Ocean. The winters in the area became wet but mild. The summers are dry but cool, due to the flow of cold air down the mountain slopes. These conditions promote the formation of moisture-laden mists that persist to this day. The climate is mild, and freezing temperatures are rare.

Extremely Slow Renewal
During the Pleistocene epoch, about one and one-half million years ago, before the ice ages, the conifers experienced an exceptional period of growth. Broadleaf trees declined in numbers, little by little, because they were less well adapted to the harsh climates. As the climate became milder, the broadleaf trees recovered their advantage. This forced the conifers to grow only in areas where their particular adaptations were still useful.

North America is home to the *Sequoia sempervirens*, called the redwood because of its cinnamon-brown bark. It is also home to

1. The sequoias are living fossils. They once grew over a much wider area than they do today. Sequoias (genera *Sequoia* and *Sequoiadendron*) currently grow only in the western part of North America (shown in the red area), and the deciduous dawn redwood, *(Metasequoia)* in a small area of China (shown in the blue area).
2. Giant sequoia *(Sequoiadendron giganteum)* in Yosemite National Park, in California **3., 4.,** and **5.** Three views of Yosemite. Yosemite is in the fog belt, which makes the growth of these giants possible. The giant sequoia can grow to be 100 meters (350 feet) tall and 25 meters (90 feet) in circumference at the base of the trunk. It also has one of the longest life spans of all the trees in the world. The enormous tree called "Grizzly Giant" in Yosemite is estimated to be between 2,500 and 3,000 years old. The name *Sequoia* was given to the tree in honor of the famous Sequoya, a Cherokee leader who created a system for writing the Cherokee language.
6. The pyramid-shaped outline of the *Sequoiadendron*, which is very different from the slender *Sequoia sempervirens*.

24

2

3

4

5   6

25

the *Sequoiadendron giganteum*, or giant sequoia. The problem of the survival of these trees in the modern world is linked to their extremely slow and inefficient reproductive success.

In the depths of the forest, the tree does not reach sexual maturity and produce fertile seeds until it is between 150 and 200 years old. The wind can carry seeds released from the cones for only short distances. The shade cast by the trees themselves makes it almost impossible for the seeds to germinate and grow. Squirrels may improve the situation to some extent by transporting the seeds and burying them in more open areas where **germination** and growth are easier. The **limiting factor** for sequoias therefore appears to be the amount of sunlight available. In open areas, in fact, cones appear on plants that are only 18 to 20 years old.

The Giants of the Plant World

Redwood trees rarely grow more than 30 to 50 kilometers (20 to 30 miles) from the Pacific coast. They generally do not appear at altitudes greater than 1,200 meters (4,000 feet) above sea level. This species includes some trees of enormous size that are nearly 120 meters (400 feet) tall and almost 12 meters (40 feet) in diameter at the base. In contrast to other conifers, the sequoia is also able to grow new branches from fallen trunks, thus regenerating the parent tree. This adaptation has proven to be very helpful, given the low rate of germination of the seeds.

Giant sequoias are native to the western slopes of the Sierra Nevada in central California. They grow in a few isolated groves distributed over approximately 400 square kilometers (150 square miles), at altitudes between 1,500 and 2,400 meters (5,000 and 7,800 feet) above sea level. The largest plant in the world is a member of this species, which at its base can have a diameter of almost 20 meters (65 feet).

The life span of sequoias is legendary. Some are more than 3,000 years old. This makes them witnesses to the great changes that have occurred on the face of the Earth. It also makes them living reminders of ancient landscapes that we can now only imagine in our minds.

1. Trunk and foliage of the coast redwood (*Sequoia sempervirens*)
2. Close-up of the typical reddish bark and the leaves of the redwood
3. Trunk and branches of the redwood
Two landscapes on the Pacific coast of California, near Big Sur **(5.)** and Plaskett Creek **(6.)**, on the edge of the Los Padres National Forest. The evergreen sequoia is called the coast redwood because of the color of its wood and its geographical distribution, which covers a narrow coastal belt from Oregon to California. It is a tree that is just as majestic as the giant sequoia and is even slightly taller. The tallest tree in the world named "Howard Libbey" is 20 meters (367 feet) high. The coast redwood also has less compact foliage. The trees live an average of 700 to 1,000 years, but individuals have been known to live for 2,600 years. The tree also grows rapidly, up to 1.2 meters (4 feet) per year in wet ground with adequate protection. Under these conditions, it can grow rapidly to a height of 30 meters (100 feet) in less than 30 years. The giant "Howard Libbey" is not particularly ancient. It is barely 500 years old.
4. The outline of *Sequoia sempervirens*, which is more slender than *Sequoiadendron*, with branches that grow lower on the trunk

1

2

THE BIRDS OF THE CONIFEROUS FORESTS

Seed-Eating Birds

Birds are some of the most visible animals in coniferous forests, as in any other type of forest. The birds' adaptations to life in the northern forests are similar to those found in other types of forests. In fact, the living conditions in the two different types of forests are quite similar. The major difference exists because the leaves in a coniferous forest are needle-shaped and are arranged all around the twigs. These factors affect the lives of the birds in several ways. For example, the birds are forced to perform acrobatic maneuvers around the branches to get to their food.

Another characteristic unique to the coniferous forests has to do with the type of plants on which the **community** of birds depend. The birds' diet has little variety and is very specialized. It consists largely of the seeds contained in pinecones. The various species have therefore become expert at removing the seeds from the scales of the pinecones or in eating buds on the branches when they are available. During certain times of year, other species base their diets on insects found in the bark of the trees.

This strict dependence on the production of conifer seeds has led to a change in the reproductive cycles of some birds so that it coincides with the maximum availability of food, regardless of the season. Parrot crossbills and white-winged crossbills depend on the **maturation cycles** of conifer seeds to reproduce. They also provide a classic example of physical adaptations to a highly specific diet. Their bills are shaped so that their upper jaw crosses their lower jaw. This arrangement enables the bird to open the scales of pinecones quickly and easily dig out the precious seeds. Such a bill is also useful for hanging and climbing on the branches, a behavior similar to that of parrots. When the production of seeds decreases due to changes in the cycles of the dominant species of trees or because of special climate conditions, many populations of birds are forced to migrate temporarily to more favorable locations. This pattern is followed by various species, such as the pine siskin (*Spinus pinus*), the hawfinch (*Coccothraustes coccothraustes*), the red or common crossbill (*Loxia curvirostra*), and the white-winged crossbill (*Loxia leucoptera*). These birds leave the northern pine forests, traveling as far south as the United States. This phenomenon is known as an **invasion**.

1

Who Stays, and Who Goes

In the summer, the northern forests echo with the calls and songs of many species, especially those of the insect-eating birds. But in the winter, these forests are abandoned until the following spring by 50 to 80 percent of the nesting species, which are unable to find sufficient food. This is the case with several warblers of the Eurasian forests, such as the willow warbler, which is abundant in summer. It is also common with the equivalent warblers in North America, which move south at the end of the summer to find the insects on which they feed. The species that stay in the winter must be able to survive a long cold season, and must feed on conifer seeds or even needles.

A strategy that differs from migration that can also be used to help the bird survive critical periods is the storing of food when it is plentiful, from August to October. For example, the large and noisy nutcracker feeds on pine seeds that it carries, up to 50 seeds at a time, in an expandable pouch under its tongue to one of its hiding places. These hiding places are located in tree stumps or crevices in the bark of trees that may be several miles from the point of collection. In addition to sustaining the nutcracker when food is scarce, these hiding places play an important part in the **ecology** of the forest. The forgotten hiding places, approximately 20 percent of the total, act as **seedbeds**.

These seedbeds contribute to the spread of various conifer species.

Another factor that limits the number of species that can survive in the northern forests is the harshness of the climate. The **adaptive response** of many birds is a dense, **downy** coat of feathers. The features provide **thermal insulation** for the animal, which must maintain a body temperature of 40° Celsius (104° F). Some birds, such as the Eurasian bullfinch, appear quite plump due to their dense coats, but actually weigh only a few grams. Some highly-specialized birds, such as the willow ptarmigan (*Lagopus lagopus*), have insulating feathers on their feet and even on their toes. These birds also adopt special behaviors to resist the cold, such as digging a burrow in the blanket of snow, where they can sleep well protected. Still other birds, such as the graceful titmouse, gather in groups of several individuals. These birds conserve their body heat by snuggling tightly up against one another.

2

1. The nutcracker (*Nucifraga caryocatactes*) is a member of the crow family that has adapted to life in coniferous forests. It feeds mainly on the seeds of the Swiss pine.

2. Among the grouse, the rock ptarmigan (*Lagopus mutus*) has unique feathers around the toes for protection from the cold. It stays above the tree line in the summer. In the winter, it sometimes hides, perfectly camouflaged by its white winter plumage, in the underbrush of the snow-covered *Abies alba*.

3. Male (red) and female (yellow-brown) crossbill, *Loxia curvirostra*. Three of the species of crossbills, **(a.)** *Loxia curvirostra*, **(b.)** *L. scotica*, and **(c.)** *L. pytyopsittacus* are perfectly adapted to eating the seeds of spruce and pine trees. When no such seeds are available, they eat the tender spring shoots of spruce and fir trees, which are shown in the background photograph.

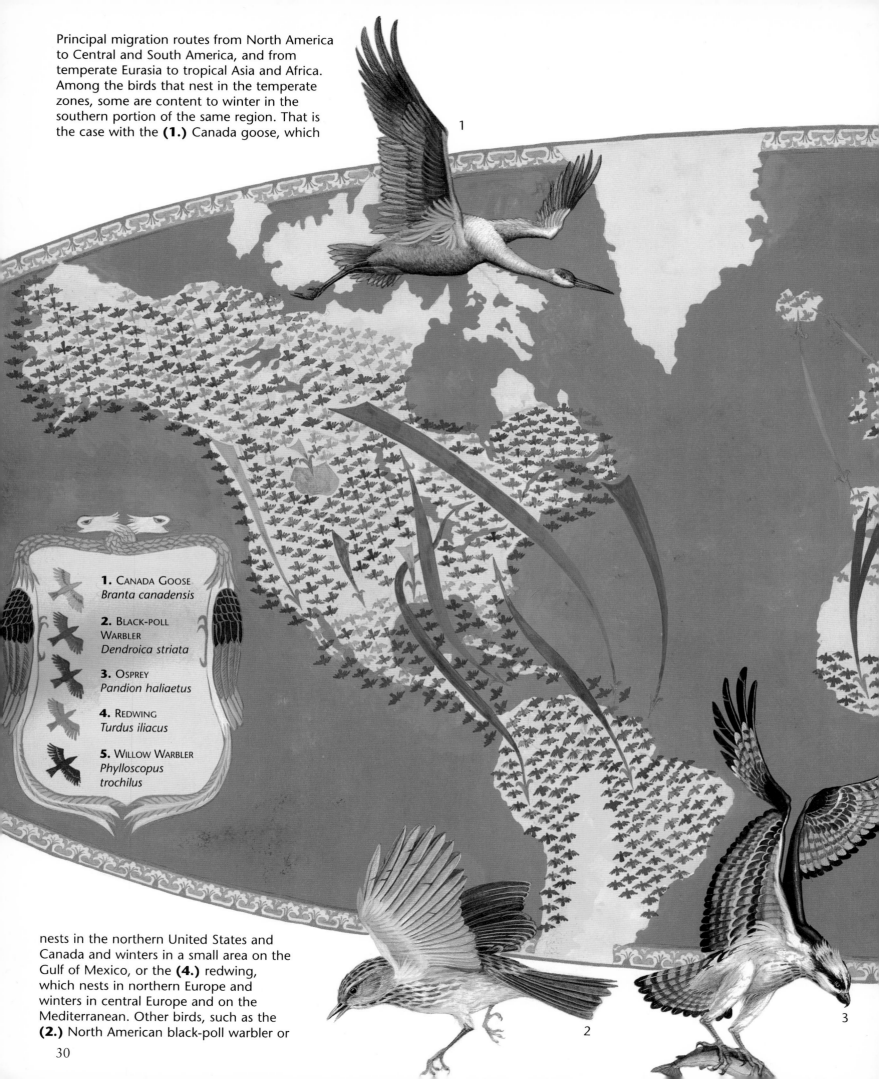

Principal migration routes from North America to Central and South America, and from temperate Eurasia to tropical Asia and Africa. Among the birds that nest in the temperate zones, some are content to winter in the southern portion of the same region. That is the case with the **(1.)** Canada goose, which

1. CANADA GOOSE
Branta canadensis

2. BLACK-POLL
WARBLER
Dendroica striata

3. OSPREY
Pandion haliaetus

4. REDWING
Turdus iliacus

5. WILLOW WARBLER
Phylloscopus trochilus

nests in the northern United States and Canada and winters in a small area on the Gulf of Mexico, or the **(4.)** redwing, which nests in northern Europe and winters in central Europe and on the Mediterranean. Other birds, such as the **(2.)** North American black-poll warbler or

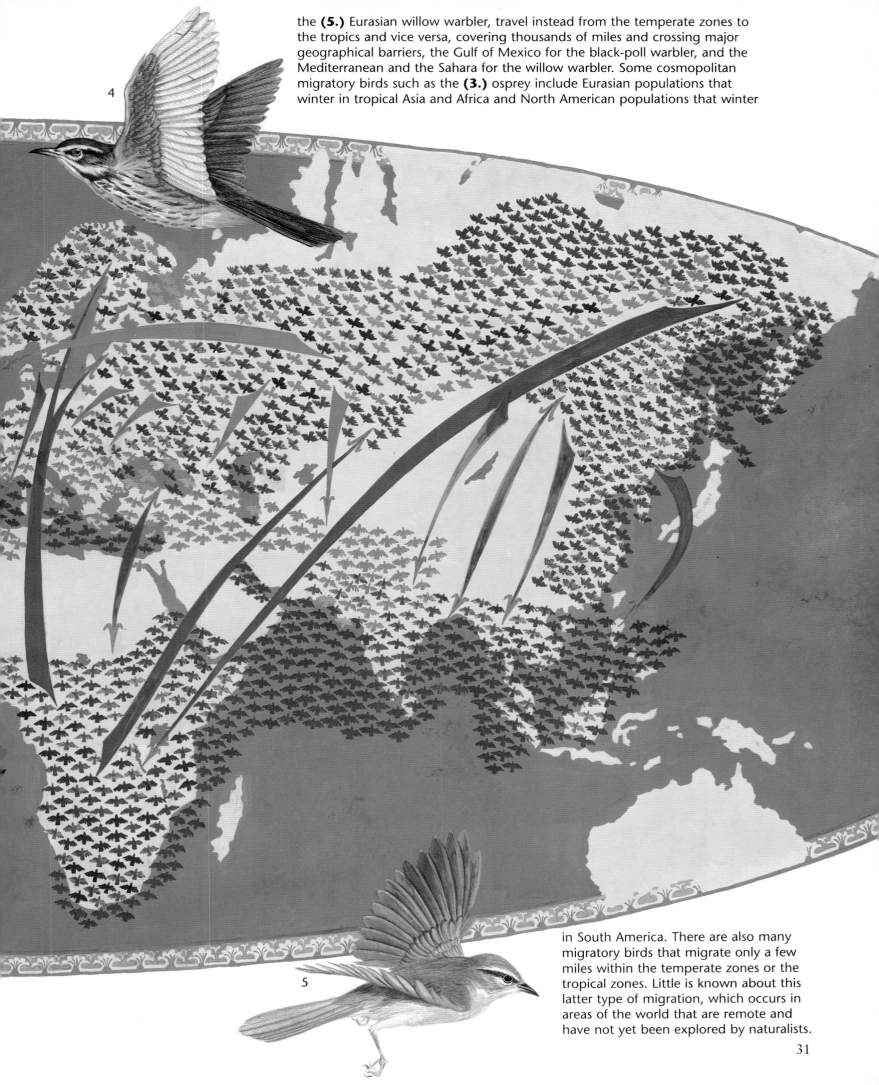

the **(5.)** Eurasian willow warbler, travel instead from the temperate zones to the tropics and vice versa, covering thousands of miles and crossing major geographical barriers, the Gulf of Mexico for the black-poll warbler, and the Mediterranean and the Sahara for the willow warbler. Some cosmopolitan migratory birds such as the **(3.)** osprey include Eurasian populations that winter in tropical Asia and Africa and North American populations that winter

in South America. There are also many migratory birds that migrate only a few miles within the temperate zones or the tropical zones. Little is known about this latter type of migration, which occurs in areas of the world that are remote and have not yet been explored by naturalists.

THE GROUSE

Birds of the Mountains and Prairies

The northern coniferous forests are typically characterized by relatively low productivity and a limited variety of food resources. Nevertheless, they are the **habitat** of choice for the Tetraonidae, a family of birds that includes grouse, ptarmigans, and prairie chickens. These birds have spectacular **plumage** and are able to survive under difficult conditions. They are medium-sized or large birds whose weight can vary from slightly more than 0.5 kilogram (1 pound) for the willow ptarmigan *(Lagopus lagopus)* to almost 5 kilograms (12 pounds) for a male **capercaillie** *(Tetrao urogallus)*.

These birds are primarily vegetarians. They are adapted to survive on an extreme diet that often includes pine needles and buds, foods not used by other animals. The digestive system of Tetraonidae is well suited for the task. It includes a very muscular **gizzard**, a portion of the stomach in which food material is ground up by small stones that the bird collects and swallows. The digestive system also has a very long **cecum**, a pouch located in the first part of the large intestine that is useful for digesting foods that are high in **cellulose**.

The members of the Tetraonidae family have very dense plumage. It is composed of a compact layer of down in direct contact with the skin that is overlaid with a coat of feathers. Even the bird's nostrils and ankles are covered with down. An additional adaptation that allows these birds to run quickly over snow-covered ground is the development of a row of stiff feathers on both sides of their toes. These feathers transform the bird's feet into veritable snowshoes.

The Male Grouse's Showy Display

Among the most majestic species in Eurasia are the capercaillie *(Tetrao urogallus)* and the black grouse *(Lyrurus tetrix)*. In North America, species include the spruce grouse *(Canachites canadensis)* and the blue grouse *(Dendragapus obscurus)*.

The spring song of the male members of the grouse family can be heard from great distances in the coniferous forests at dawn and at dusk. Sitting on the ground, on a stump, or on an exposed branch, the male grouse gather in groups and emit shrill calls, clicking noises, and intense **trills** to attract the females. The males extend their necks to increase the resonance, spreading their wings downward and opening their tails in the

shape of a fan. When they are caught up in their courting, it almost seems as if the males of some species can no longer see or hear, so intense is their concentration on their display. The females, which are smaller and less showy, arrive at this arena or dancing ground. Their presence causes the males to produce even more spectacular displays.

The male black grouse, which is actually dark blue-black with contrasting white feathers, red **caruncles**, and an elegant lyre-shaped tail, gather at dawn in forest clearings called **leks**, or dancing grounds. The males engage each other in ritual combat. The successful males are those that manage to occupy and defend territories in the center of the arena. Only these males can mate with the females who visit the arena to select a father for their future offspring.

The **sociosexual system** of the grouse does not result in a stable **pair-bond**. Nor does it require the father to provide any care for the chicks. The male's only task is to supply "good genes," thereby guaranteeing the quality of future generations. The female does everything else by herself. She builds the nest, **incubates** the eggs, and raises the chicks.

This type of **reproductive strategy** may be designed to bring together animals that are otherwise spread thinly throughout the large forests, where the food supply is poor. Evolution may have gradually favored the males that were showiest and capable of putting on the most spectacular displays. Evolution may have also favored the females who became increasingly **camouflaged** and more modest.

A display of black grouse *(Lyrurus tetrix)* on a dancing ground at dawn on a February morning. The males challenge one another, while the females watch closely to select a mate. The competition among the males is the essential element that stimulates the females. If at least two males are not present on the dancing ground, the females will completely ignore any single males who have not won at least one challenge.

BIRDS OF PREY

Great-Winged Hunters

The northern forests have winged rulers of the daytime and nighttime skies. The sky during the day is ruled by the goshawks and the sparrow hawks. The night sky is the realm of a small group of owls that are particularly well adapted to life in the taiga.

The unchallenged master of the daytime sky is the powerful goshawk (*Accipiter gentilis*). The supreme master of the night sky is the great gray owl (*Strix nebulosa*). Both the goshawk and the great gray owl weigh about 1 kilogram (2.5 pounds). Both types of birds live in the Northern Hemisphere, in Scandinavia, European Russia, Siberia, and North America.

The Spotted Owl

To the south of the territory occupied by the great gray owl, in the humid forests of the western United States, there is another, smaller species of the genus *Strix*. This owl, which has been in the news often, is the northern spotted owl (*Strix occidentalis*). The northern spotted owl is at the center of a fierce political and legal debate *Owls v. Jobs*, which has pitted the timber industry against environmentalists in the United States. The northern spotted owl needs a habitat of old-growth forests with many large trees. The bird disappears if too much timber is harvested.

If we can look beyond the heated arguments of both sides, there is no doubt that it has been possible to preserve magnificent forests that are extremely rich in plant and animal life. For example, forests in the western United States are also the home of the small pygmy owl (*Glaucidium gnoma)*, the Kennicott's owl (*Otus kennicottii*), and the flammulated owl (*Otus flammeolus*), to mention just a few among the nocturnal birds of prey.

Northern Owls

The arctic and subarctic territory of the great gray owl is similar to that of the boreal owl (*Aegolius funereus*), a species that is well protected from the rigors of the climate by its extremely dense plumage. Hidden among the thick Norway spruce, both in North America and in Eurasia, this plump little owl is rarely seen. It lets its presence be known by its characteristic song, which echoes through the forest during the mating season.

Another small owl that is distributed throughout the northern forests around the world is the hawk owl (*Surnia ulula*). Similar to the sparrow hawk in both its appearance and its predatory habits, it is not a typical night hunter. Both in northern Eurasia and in North America, this species inhabits the same forest environments as goshawks and sparrow hawks. Just like the hawks, it prefers sites with easy access to clearings. It is one of the few species of small owls that is also active during the day. It perches in wait on the tops of tall conifers and swoops down on smaller birds, starting acrobatic chases through the trees. At night, it hunts small mammals on the floor of the forest.

Winged Hunter-Acrobats

The true sparrow hawks and goshawks hunt both mammals and birds. They dart among the trunks of the trees and emerge into clearings in the northern forests for only moments at a time.

These Falconiformes, or diurnal birds of prey of the family Accipitridae, specialize in a type of hunting that takes advantage of their thickly forested environment. Their attacks are usually launched from an observation point that is not exposed, but which offers the bird a good view of its surroundings. Often such sites are available at the edges of a clearing. The silence of their flight,

The *Owls v. Jobs* controversy in the United States between promoters of industrial development at all costs and defenders of the natural environment began with the destruction of the habitat of the northern spotted owl (*Strix occidentalis*). This owl lives only in the old-growth coniferous forests on the west coast, near the border of Canada. The situation has highlighted the need for legal intervention to protect some of the most extraordinary ecosystems on our planet, even though all the data that might identify the environmental damage caused by industrial development may not yet be available.

the surprise effect of their attack, and their strength and gracefulness often make for a successful hunt.

Shy, unnoticed, and rarely vocal, goshawks and sparrow hawks (genus *Accipiter*) are sighted infrequently. Their activity becomes

Their nests are always hidden by the dense foliage. During the incubation period, the male delivers enough food to the nest for its mate. Later, he also brings food for the chicks for a certain period after they hatch.

The two sexes of forest hawks are visibly

Competition between the partners for food is reduced because the prey captured is proportional to the bird's size. This fact would also reduce the aggression between the two birds of the pair and make possible a more efficient use of resources. Such a distinct spe-

female

1

male

2

female

4

male

5

3

As a result of the different sizes of the two sexes in both the goshawk, *Accipiter gentilis* (**1.** and **2.)** and the sparrow hawk, *Accipiter nisus* (**4.** and **5.**), the range of potential prey available to just these two winged predators of the coniferous forests is vast.
3. Among the hunting techniques used by the versatile goshawk are attacks from below and from above against birds, and attack from above against mammals. Birds are attacked from directly behind, which is the one blind spot in their otherwise wide-angle vision. Mammals or ground-nesting birds are surprised by a sudden dive from a tree or shrub.

readily visible only during the courtship period. At this time, the members of the pair engage in spectacular aerial courtship displays. Once they have formed their pairbond, the male and female begin building a new nest of sticks and twigs or restore an old nest site located high up in tall conifers.

different in size. The female is much larger than the male. There are several explanations for the evolution of these two body types, which are apparent in birds that feed on highly mobile prey, such as other birds. For example, different sizes reduce the overlap in their respective food supplies.

cialization also increases reproductive success. The time at which the female leaves the nest containing the growing nestlings and returns to hunting is when the young require a greater supply of food than in the early phases of their development, when only the male provides their food.

The Eurasian eagle owl (*Bubo bubo*), shown here in a nineteenth-century engraving, is the largest of the nocturnal predators and is one of the most powerful predatory birds in existence. In spite of relatively small populations, it is found over a wide area and can survive and reproduce in various types of forests. It requires a refuge far from civilization, in a ravine or another relatively inaccessible area, where there are cavities suitable for building its nest.

37

THE CERVIDAE FAMILY

Animals of Marshes and Snow-Covered Landscapes

In the coniferous forests there is no lack of food to appeal to the appetites of **herbivores**. The bark, **foliage**, tender shoots, fruits, berries, lichens, mushrooms, and other products of the lower layer of the northern forests are the basic diet of some of the larger members of the Cervidae family.

This family includes deer and elk that frequent taiga environments for at least part of the year. The reindeer, called the caribou in the United States, the elk, and the moose are animals that can move easily over marshy and snow-covered ground due to their wide hooves. These animals prefer areas where the dense forest is interrupted by clearings and marshes, which they use to escape the swarms of stinging mosquitoes that breed during the brief arctic summer. These animals are also insulated by thick coats that allow them to survive the frigid arctic winters with a minimal loss of body heat.

The Giant of the Cervidae

The genuine giant of the Cervidae family is *Alces alces*, called the elk in Europe and the moose in North America. The name "elk" in North America is used to designate a different animal, the wapiti, which is closely related to the red deer of Europe.

The male moose often grows to a length of 3.4 meters (11 feet), a height of more than 1.8 meters (6 feet) at the shoulder, and weighs almost a ton. The large head, with its wide brow and fleshy upper lip, is decorated with antlers shaped like palm leaves. The antlers may weigh as much as 22.7 kilograms (50 pounds). They fall off and grow back every year. The moose has a distinctive bulky profile, an impression that is emphasized by its short neck and massive trunk. This giant's territory extends throughout the Northern forests around the world. To a

great extent, the moose's territory is the same as the area occupied by the coniferous forests. These areas include: Scandinavia, Russia, Siberia, Manchuria and Mongolia, Alaska, Canada, and the northern United States.

In contrast to the other members of the Cervidae family, the moose has rather solitary habits. Isolated individuals, always wary and constantly on their guard, roam safely in the underbrush. They graze mostly at dusk and rest to **ruminate** during the middle of the day. Their behavior changes greatly in late summer, when the mating season begins. The males, with their antlers in full splendor, roar through the forest seeking females of reproductive age. They remain with the females for a brief period following mating, during which time they continue to seek other available mates. Moose calves remain with their mothers for a long time and occasionally gather in small, mixed herds in the winter.

In the summer, moose prefer to feed on water plants, swamp grasses, and the grasses that grow in clearings. During the winter, they are forced to eat buds, fresh shoots, and the bark of woody plants and shrubs in the underbrush.

The Large Herds of the North

The Eurasian reindeer and the North American caribou *(Rangifer tarandus)* are highly social animals. They are generally considered to belong to two very distinct populations of the same species. Their diet is somewhat different from and more specific than that of the moose. In contrast to the other members of the Cervidae family, reindeer of both sexes typically have antlers, but the antlers are less developed in the females. Inhabitants of the tundra in the summer, they take refuge in the winter in the more sheltered southern coniferous forests.

The caribou's famous long migrations, from 640 to 800 kilometers (400 to 500 miles) are truly spectacular. Herds of tens of thousands of individuals file along traditional migration routes. They cross streams, rivers, rocky plains, and snow-covered grasslands. Their diet changes greatly during this journey. From a diet based on the grasses of the arctic tundra, it changes to a diet of mostly reindeer moss (*Cladonia rangiferina*), as well as leafy lichens that climb conifers, mosses, and buds of plants that grow among the underbrush. Because of the special design of their snowshoe-like hooves, reindeer and caribou can walk without sinking into the snow. They even dig into the snow to find the naturally frozen lichens.

The reindeer has been one of the most important resources for the inhabitants of extreme northern Eurasia for tens of thousands of years. Some reindeer are semidomesticated in herds that are left to roam freely. Many are fully domesticated. The Lapps, for example, use the reindeer as pack animals, riding animals, and for pulling sleds, as well as for their meat, hide, fat, wool, milk, tendons, and bones, which are made into utensils. The Inuit still hunt the wild animals, following the migration routes and forcing caribou herds into fatal ambushes, as they have done for hundreds of years.

1. Lichens *(Cladonia stellaris)* in a Finnish forest. This species, which is dominant in the underbrush of Scandinavian coniferous forests, is frequently eaten by reindeer and caribou.
2. A male moose and its hoofprint on a muddy shore of the Baltic Sea, in Finland. The large moose is still a species found over wide areas of the Scandinavian forests. In Scandinavia alone, there is a population of hundreds of thousands of individuals.

1. Adult male caribou *(Rangifer tarandus),* which is shedding the "velvet" of its branched horns, called antlers. **2.** The antlers are rubbed against the bark of trees, which clearly show the traces of the animal's activity in late autumn.

4. Reindeer moss *(Cladonia rangiferina)* is an important element in the diet of reindeer and caribou during their migrations.

3. Reindeer *(Rangifer tarandus)* in the winter snow of Lapland
5. Migrating herd of caribou in the Canadian Northwest Territories. Reindeer and caribou are different populations of the same species that live in the Eurasian tundra and in North America, respectively. The main difference between the two populations is that, while caribou have remained strictly wild, reindeer have been domesticated for tens of thousands of years and are now under the direct control of the Lapps. Nevertheless, both reindeer and caribou migrate regularly twice a year from the arctic tundra to the taiga and vice versa. In this case, humans have had to adapt to the habits of the animals, rather than the other way around. In North America, the Inuit have not domesticated the caribou. The caribou are still hunted and not raised as livestock.

PREDATORY MAMMALS

The Wolverine

The most characteristic predator of the northern forests is also the largest ground-dwelling member of the weasel family in the world: the wolverine (*Gulo gulo*). The wolverine's territory coincides with the Eurasian and North American taiga. Its favorite prey are reindeer and small caribou. It also hunts small mammals that scamper over the blanket of conifer needles, as well as birds of all sizes. Wolverines will eat **carrion** of all types. They are also content to eat berries and fresh shoots, if nothing better is to be found.

The wolverine is one of the strongest carnivores in the temperate zone. It could easily put up a good fight against a wildcat or a wolf if it had the unlikely idea of attacking one. The wolverine is often considered an enemy by humans because it is a predator of other animals that are considered desirable. The wolverine also represents one of the few animals that is well adapted to movement on snow-covered ground. From this point of view, it is similar to the legendary sable (*Martes zibellina*), a smaller Siberian member of the weasel family, which is famous for its extraordinarily luxurious fur.

The wolverine is awkward and uncomfortable when it has to track its prey on ground that is not covered by snow. In that case, it prefers to fill up on shrews, lemmings, small rodents, and the eggs and chicks of ground-nesting birds. But the wolverine's genuine athletic talents emerge when it tracks large herds of reindeer or caribou over the snow-covered ground. Its large, sturdy paws no longer seem oversized, but keep it from sinking into the snow as it runs. Much stronger than bears or wolves, the wolverine seizes its prey by the back of the neck and digs in with its fearful claws and long canine teeth. Although it is only about 66 to 89 centimeters (26 to 35 inches) long, about 40 to 50 centimeters (16 to 20 inches) high, and weighs a maximum of 23 to 40 kilograms (50 to 88 pounds), it can bring down animals much larger than itself.

Wolverines lead solitary lives, each controlling its own territory but without establishing a permanent den. Only the females, which are smaller than the males, take refuge

The wolverine *(Gulo gulo),* which next to the bear and the wolf is the strongest carnivore of the large northern forests. It specializes in tracking large prey over snow-covered ground, as does the lynx. (The two illustrations are not drawn to the same scale.) The lynx is significantly larger— 86 to 112 centimeters (34 to 44 inches) in length compared to 66 to 89 centimeters (26 to 35 inches) for the wolverine. The lynx *(Lynx lynx)* hunts smaller prey, such as hares and wildfowl, relying on a noiseless approach followed by a sudden and unexpected attack.

in natural cavities or in nests dug in the snow. They use the nests to give birth to litters of two to five cubs. The bond with the mother lasts for another 2 years. In their territories, which are temporary, wolverines store food. The food is preserved by the freezing temperatures. Their strength and climbing ability allow them to carry an entire carcass, even a reindeer, up into a tree, where the carcass is hung over a branch until it has been fully consumed.

Wolverines are active hunters, but they are also extremely efficient **scavengers**. They frequently trail large herds of migrating reindeer, preying on young, old, or sick animals. They also follow bears or packs of wolves, cleaning up the remainders of their catches.

Bears, Wolves, and Wildcats

Predators roam silently through the dark underbrush carpeted by dried needles. The brown bear (*Ursus arctos*), with its many geographical variants, is really an omnivore, but it sometimes preys directly on large animals. The wolf (*Canis lupus*) is a more frequent carnivore. Like the bear, the wolf ranges throughout the belt of coniferous forests, from the broadleaf forests to the open tundra.

The most elegant and majestic predator of the northern forests is a large wildcat that has extremely acute vision and a noiseless tread: the lynx (*Lynx lynx*). The lynx's fur is extremely dense. It is light brown with shades of red and has dark spots. The lynx's unique traits include tufts of stiff fur that grow from its large ears and a sort of **goatee** that hangs from its neck.

According to recent studies, the tufts on the lynx's ears seem to act as antennae to collect sounds and locate their source. The lynx's hunting methods and movements are similar to those of the domestic cat. Their sneaky and noiseless tread is made possible by the thick coat of fur and the large pads on the soles of their feet. The pads allow the lynx to move easily over snow-covered, icy, or even rocky ground. Each lynx hunts in a defined territory, the size of which depends on the available food resources. The boundaries of each territory are marked by small, prominently placed piles of **excrement** and scratches in the bark of trees made by the animal's claws. During the mating season, the females travel in search of a male. After mating, they return to their usual territories. The lynx rarely preys on animals larger than itself. It prefers to hunt birds, rabbits and hares, rats, and herbivores no larger than a small deer.

2

1. The cougar (*Felis concolor*), after the disappearance of the jaguar, is the only survivor along with the lynx of the big North American cats.
2. The sable (*Martes zibellina*) is a Siberian species closely related to the marten. It is almost legendary for its extraordinarily soft fur.
3. and **4.** The grizzly (*Ursus arctos horribilis*) is the giant-size version of the European brown bear (*Ursus arctos arctos*). This carnivore has been almost exterminated in the United States, but survives in Alaska and Canada. It can weigh up to 794 kilograms (1,750 pounds), but it still climbs trees with skill, like the cub shown in the top photo. It feeds on a vast range of prey, including migrating salmon in the rivers and streams of Alaska.

4

THE DETERIORATION OF THE NORTHERN FORESTS

An Overexploited Ecosystem

The northern belt of coniferous forests is still fairly intact in terms of the geographical territory it covers. This is true especially when compared to broadleaf forests or **tropical forests**. Along its southern edges, where the human population density is greatest, there has been some loss of territory. However, to the north, the forest has remained intact. It is protected by the harsh climate and the permanently frozen ground that makes agriculture impossible. Nor are the harsh northern climates attractive as industrial sites.

To those who remember the taiga as it was only 50 years ago, it is obvious that even this ecosystem has been profoundly changed. Many species of animals have become scarce for a variety of reasons. Many forests have been overharvested by the timber industry, frequently with disastrous results for the populations not only of large animals, but also of small birds. Recent research in Sweden has shown that the **population density** of the Siberian titmouse has decreased by 90 percent where the age of the forest has been reduced by excessively frequent cutting. If that were not enough, the surviving animals and plants face an even more mysterious enemy from the sky: **acid rain.**

Poison from the Sky

The Northern Hemisphere forests are completely defenseless against acid rain. Although the forested areas in the north are not decreasing in size and there has even been a reversal of the trend to clear-cut more land in recent years, the forests are deteriorating because of the declining average age of the trees and the increasingly serious effects of acid rain.

The countries most severely affected by this phenomenon are those which, on account of the global circulation of the atmosphere, are exposed to clouds of acid produced in other regions. The effects of acid rain are very apparent in Canada, Scandinavia, and north-central Europe. In Germany, about 50 percent of the forests have been affected to varying degrees. The damage to the conifers, and to all the trees in general, is of two types. The damage affects the foliage directly, or gradually changes the chemical composition of the soil.

1. Fire in the Boise National Forest, in Idaho
2. Disastrous effects of acid rain on a coniferous forest in the former Czechoslovakia. Acid rain is a relatively recent environmental problem. It is caused by rain that washes acid

04.08.92
IDAHO/USA: INCENDIE A
BOISE NATIONAL FOREST

1

from an atmosphere severely polluted by industrial discharges from power plants in the industrialized areas of Europe and North America. The rain is changed into a solution of hazardous substances that slowly destroys thousands of acres of forests. High-tech, and therefore very expensive, solutions are being studied to combat this phenomenon, assuming that it can be reversed at all.

2

TREES WITH ACID RAIN
DAMAGE. CZECHOSLOVAKIA, POLLUTION

grazia neri srl

Kodachrome
FILM

The accumulation of poisonous substances on leaves causes **macroscopic changes**. It destroys the **chlorophyll**, thus causing the death of the leaves. In conifers, the tips of individual needles turn a light brown color, which is a sign of the **necrosis** of the needle. Younger leaves show signs of premature aging, which interferes with the leaf replacement cycles. But the symptoms are not always that obvious. The damage may only become apparent over long periods, as the tree shows a general decline in health. Reduced fertility and a reduction in the size of the pollen grains are also common effects of acid rain.

Poison from the Land

The attack of acid rain continues from below in the form of the acidification of the soil by substances dissolved in water or in the air. The soils of the coniferous forests are already acid. This makes them vulnerable to more acidification, because they cannot neutralize acid substances beyond a certain limit. These conditions are harmful not only to the large trees exposed to the action of the acid rain, but also to the plants of the underbrush, including lichens and fungi. Some species die, and others survive. In either case, the changes to the environment are severe and irreversible, at least until the causes of acid rain can be eliminated.

Top three photos: View of the Aletsch Forest in the Canton of Valais, in Switzerland. It covers about 304 hectares (750 acres) on the edges of the northern moraine slopes of the Aletsch Glacier at an average altitude of 2,134 meters (7,000 feet). This rich forest is composed of 70 percent arolla or Swiss pines, 20 percent larch, and 5 percent red spruces. It has enjoyed total protection for the last 50 years, during which time the number of trees has tripled from 18,839 in 1942 to 61,471 in 1982. The forest has recently suffered a high mortality rate among young trees, which are being eaten by grazing animals. In any case, because both the Swiss pines and the larches require much open space around them to grow, the forest is very open and bright. This allows the growth of a lush underbrush of shrubs in which the rhododendron and whortleberry abound.

Bottom four photos: Views in the Derborance Forest, also in the Swiss Canton of Valais, and considered the last remaining virgin forest of silver fir and Norway spruce in the Alps. The steep mountain terrain, its distance from inhabited areas, and the abundance of tall trees compared to forests at lower altitudes have kept timber companies and cattle herders away from this forest. Above all, it is the tragic events that occurred in 1714 and 1749, when two gigantic landslides sent 8,500 cubic meters (300,000 cubic feet) of rock roaring down the mountain, destroying Alpine huts and killing residents, that has kept people away. Since then, the forest has remained undisturbed. Its current life cycle is approximately 300 years, with immense trees that grow side by side, live, die, topple, and leave open spaces that let in more sunlight, allowing seeds to germinate on the rotting wood of fallen trunks.

THE DEEP GREEN PLANET

A flying saucer observing the Earth from many points—over the Amazon, Siberia, or Borneo, for example—would see a rolling sea of treetops. Forests are the fundamental environment of our planet. They are the environment that dominates and persists over time, following the colonization of Earth by living things. In a climate that is not too cold or dry, the result of colonization will be a forest of some kind. Whether deciduous broadleaf or evergreen, mixed or coniferous, tropical or temperate, it will still be a forest.

The difference between town and countryside is decided by humans. If nature was left to its own devices, the difference would disappear in a sea of trees, like the famous temples of Cambodia. Apart from the oceans, the tundra, and the deserts, the whole planet is, will be, or would be covered with forest. In a forest environment, the terrestrial ecosystems draw breath. Their continuous labors cease, and they finally rest in a stable, durable form that is resistant to change. The concept of the town and the countryside has no future, except in the hands of people who decide it on the basis of their needs. Forests are the true future of the planet. When they are felled, burned, and uprooted, it is that very future that is being destroyed.

Ecologists say that forests are climax environments. Climax environments are stable, well defined, and balanced with a wide range of different species, microclimates, and subsystems. The destruction of forests means destroying something that was established and lasting, and replacing it with something new, unstable, and temporary. The destruction of even small areas of a large forest means the extermination of native species. It also means the wiping out of small worlds with unique characteristics. The destruction of the world's great forests at the current rate—150,000 square kilometers (58,000 square miles) each year—means the destruction of the planet itself. It means increasing the danger of total collapse day by day. Whatever the outcome, our planet without its forests will be a different world: one languishing in the memories of its past splendors. Let's hope that terrible day is still a long way off, and better still, that it never arrives.

RENATO MASSA

GLOSSARY

acidify To lower the pH of a substance

acid rain Precipitation having a lower than normal pH that results when water vapor in the air combines with chemical substances to form acids

adaptation A process in which a species changes with environmental conditions

adaptive response A change in the characteristics of an animal or plant population. It is determined by natural selection, and results in the adaptation of external or genetic traits suited to a new environmental situation.

alkaline Substance having a pH greater than 7; a base

angiosperm A plant that forms its seeds in flowers

aril Seed-covering of the seeds of some conifers, generally having a fleshy appearance

ash Any tree of the genus *Fraxinus* of the olive family with feather-shaped leaves, thin bark, and gray branchlets

aspen Any of several poplars in Europe and North America that have leaves that flutter in the lightest wind due to their flat leaf stems

broadleaf tree Type of tree in a temperate climate that has leaves that are not needles

buttresses Roots that develop out of a tree trunk above the soil and provide a supplementary support for the tree

calcium A silver-white metallic element

camouflage The disguising of something, especially to make it look like what is around them

canopy A self-contained environment created by the high branches of forest trees

capercaillie A large grouse that lives in Eurasia

carbohydrates Any of the group of organic compounds composed of carbon, hydrogen, and oxygen, including sugars and starches

carrion The dead bodies or carcasses of animals that have been killed by predators or have died from natural causes

caruncle A fleshy outgrowth similar to a bird's wattle

cecum A pouch in the large intestine of birds that is used in the digestion of cellulose

cellulose A carbohydrate used by plants as the skeletal structure of the cell wall. It generally cannot be used as food by animals, except for animals such as termites or ruminants.

chlorophyll A green pigment present in plant cells that is essential for photosynthesis

community All the populations living in the same area

conifer Any tree that produces uncovered seeds in cones, such as a pine or fir

coniferous forest Region dominated by trees that produce their seeds in cones

deciduous broadleaf trees Trees that lose their leaves during parts of the year, usually fall and winter

dioecious Plant having reproductive structures of only one sex, male or female

down General term used to designate the small, dense feathers of birds that provide a dense covering for the body and sometimes even the feet and to protect the bird against the cold

drainage Elimination of excess water by runoff

ecologist One who studies ecology

ecology The study of the relationships between organisms and their environments

epiphytes Common name for nonparasitic plants that grow on other plants

everglades Marshy areas having many small islands

evergreen Plants that have a continuous growth cycle and do not generally lose all their leaves at once

excrement Waste discharged from the body

false fruit A fleshy seed-covering that does not form from modifications of the ovary

foliage Leaves

fungi Kingdom of single-celled and many-celled organisms that have nuclei and are able to carry out photosynthesis

germination The initial stages in the growth of a seed

gizzard Part of the stomach of a bird in which food matter is ground up with the aid of small stones the bird swallows

goatee A small pointed or tufted beard

gymnosperm A plant that produces naked seeds, such as the ginkgoes, the Gnetaceae, the cycads, and several extinct classes

habitat The place where an organism lives

herbivore An animal that feeds only on plants and plant parts

hermaphroditic Individual having both male and female reproductive structures

incubate To sit on eggs so they will hatch by the warmth of the body

inflorescence A group of flowers that grow together along a single or branched axis with various forms

invasion The migration of birds when they are forced to leave an area temporarily in order to find better places to feed

juniper Any shrub or tree of the cypress family that has needlike leaves and cones that resemble berries

larch A conifer in the genus *Larix* that sheds its needles in the winter

latitude Distance in degrees north or south of the equator

lek Display arena of the males of particular species of mammals or birds that practice a unique sociosexual system that does not entail long-term relationships between males and females. The males are selected by the females solely on the basis of their characteristics and are evaluated on their behavior in the arena.

limiting factor Any environmental factor that restricts the presence or growth of a species

macroscopic changes Transformations that are easily visible

magnesium A soft, silvery metallic element needed by living things

mangrove A type of tropical tree that sends out many prop roots

maturation cycle The process of becoming mature

mineral salts Inorganic substances that plants need to grow that include compounds of nitrogen, phosphorus, magnesium, potassium, and other necessary elements in small quantities

monoecious Hermaphroditic plants

moraine An accumulation of stones and earth that was carried and deposited by a glacier

moss Tiny spore-producing plant that lacks true roots, stems, and leaves

necrosis Death of tissue

nutrients Chemical substances living things need for growth, energy, and repair

order A category of classification of life above the family and below the class

organic Containing carbon

outgrowth Something that grows directly out of something else

ovary The female reproductive organ

pair-bond A relationship that involves having a single mate for a period of time

parasite An organism that feeds on the tissues or fluids of another organism, called the host, usually causing some harm to the organism

petiole A slender stem that supports the blade of a leaf

phosphorus A nonmetallic element needed by living things

photosynthesis Food-making process of plants in which carbon dioxide and water are joined to produce glucose, oxygen, and energy

plumage The feathers of a bird

pneumatophores The submerged roots of the bald cypress that are unique because they function as respiratory organs for the tree

podzol Soil typical of Northern Hemisphere areas with a cold climate. It is characterized by an ashy-gray color, a low humus content, and covers the black and red underlying soils that are richer in organic substances. Podzol is particularly suitable for the growth of conifers.

podzolization The process of development of podzol soil

pollen Spores produced by male reproductive cells and contained in pollen sacs in the male part of the flower, called the stamen

population density The number of organisms of a species per unit area

potassium A metallic element needed for the synthesis of proteins in living things

pseudodrupe False fruit that contains the seeds of the yews or podocarps

reproductive strategy Method for reproducing and raising offspring that will ensure the existence of a species

resin An organic substance made up of tannins and terpenes that forms in plant secretions and discourages other organisms from boring into the plant tissue

ruminant Suborder of mammals that have the ability to digest cellulose

ruminate To chew again what has already been chewed and swallowed

scale A modified leaf of a conifer that supports and partly surrounds a seed

scavenger An organism that feeds on refuse or carrion

seedbed A bed of soil prepared for planting seeds

self-fertilization Union of male and female reproductive cells originating from the same hermaphroditic individual

sequoia One of two huge coniferous California trees of the bald cypress family

sociosexual system Organization of the social and sexual relationships within a population in relation to reproductive activity

strobilus Set of scales that bear seeds in the conifers, representing the final product of the mature inflorescence

subarctic Characteristic of regions immediately outside of the arctic circle

subtropics Regions bordering the tropical zone

taiga Coniferous forest of the northernmost regions of the Northern Hemisphere

tannin Colored substance present in various parts of a plant that are relatively indigestible and discourage herbivores from eating the plant

temperate rain forest Type of forest in which conifers prevail that is characterized by temperatures and precipitation that are considered moderate throughout the year

temperate zone The climate zone located approximately between 40 and 60 degrees latitude that is characterized by having moderate weather and climate conditions

terpene A chemical substance contained in the tissues of many plants that among other things helps protect the plant from ingestion by herbivores

thermal insulation The ability to prevent the transfer of heat

topographical slope The upward or downward slant of the Earth's physical or natural features

trill The alternation of two musical notes; warble

tropical forest An evergreen or deciduous forest that grows under conditions of suitable temperature and rainfall

true fruit A fleshy seed-covering that forms from the ovary

tundra A treeless environment of the extreme north that includes areas in which the ground is permanently frozen

underbrush Plants such as shrubs, bushes, and mosses that grow near ground level in a forest

whortleberry A European blueberry

yew Any of a genus *Taxus* of evergreen trees and shrubs with stiff linear leaves and fruits with a fleshy aril

FURTHER READING

Brimner, Larry D. *Unusual Friendships: Symbiosis in the Animal World*. Watts, 1993
Costa-Pace, Rosa. *Protecting Our Forests*. Chelsea House, 1994
Dowden, Anne O. *The Blossom on the Bough: A Book of Trees*. Ticknor & Fields, 1994
Gallant, Roy A. *Earth's Vanishing Forests*. Macmillan, 1992
Ganeri, Anita. *Forests*. Raintree Steck-Vaughn, 1997
Garassino, Alessandro. *Plants: Origins and Evolution*. Raintree Steck-Vaughn, 1995
Greenaway, Theresa. *Fir Trees*. Raintree Steck-Vaughn, 1990
Greenaway, Theresa. *Woodland Trees*. Raintree Steck-Vaughn, 1991
Hester, Nigel. *The Living Tree*. Watts, 1990
Keirns, Johanna L. *The Cone Connection: A Guide to Cone-Bearing Trees in California's Mountains*.
   Virgilio Integrated, 1992
Legget, Jeremy. *Dying Forests*. Marshall Cavendish, 1991
Lucas, Eileen. *Everglades*. Raintree Steck-Vaughn, 1995
Raintree Steck-Vaughn Staff. *Atlas of the Environment*. Coote, Roger, ed. Raintree Steck-Vaughn, 1992
Walker, Jane. *Vanishing Habitats and Species*. Watts, 1993

PICTURE CREDITS

INDEX